Stop F...ng Tweeting and go the F...k to Sleep, Mr. President

Written and illustrated by
John Spreincer McKellyanne Huckamucci

ISBN: 978-0-9885273-2-4

First edition November 2017.

This book isn't affiliated with, authorized by or endorsed by Akashic Books or
Adam Mansbach, the brilliant author of the book from which this parody takes
cues. You can find *his* work over at adammansbach.com.

Dedicated to everyone with a shitty boss who makes you look bad no matter what you freaking do and stains your professional reputation for life even though it's not my fault this shit happened and this probably was my only chance to work at the White House so what was I supposed to do, say no? YOU SAY NO you brave keyboard warrior with 40 Twitter followers, most of them porn bots who will never love you back because you spend half your workday resenting your jackass co-worker who makes more than you despite spending all day playing Clash of Clans, sound on with no headphones, in the cube next to you and no one ever says shit about how unfair that is, least of all you. At least I get to be on TV

The fox nestles close to his friends—
Wait, hold on, this episode's a repeat.
You watched it already this afternoon.
Mr. President, it's time to go to sleep.

The windows are dark in D.C.
Your staff huddles down to silently weep.
I'll read you one last story from Infowars
If you promise you'll then go to sleep.

The eagles who **BEEP BEEP**
Ah, dammit, a text from Steve.
Your phone didn't unmute itself, sir.
That's bullshit, stop lying.
Put it down, and go the fuck to sleep.

The wind whis—where the fuck are you going.
Lay down. You've got a schedule to keep.
I don't care what ESPN said about you.
Your phone's out of battery and, like you, it needs some fucking sleep.

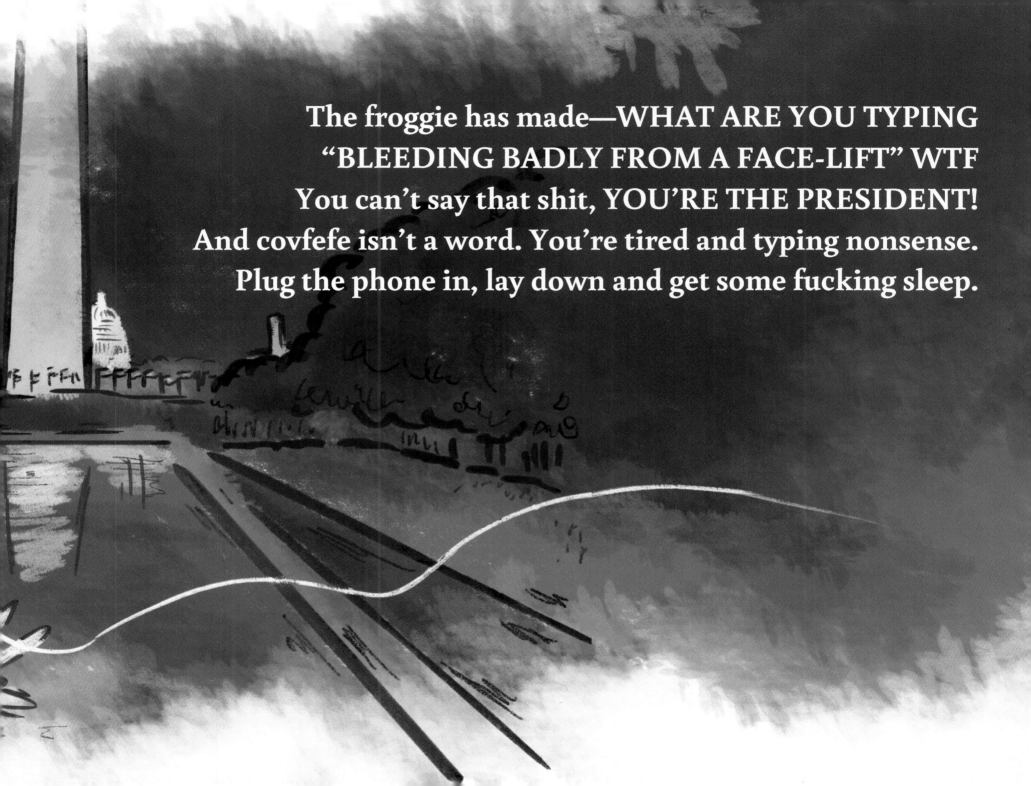

The froggie has made—WHAT ARE YOU TYPING
"BLEEDING BADLY FROM A FACE-LIFT" WTF
You can't say that shit, YOU'RE THE PRESIDENT!
And covfefe isn't a word. You're tired and typing nonsense.
Plug the phone in, lay down and get some fucking sleep.

The owls fly fo—oh Jesus you can't say that, that is so fucking racist—
WHAT DO YOU MEAN "HOW IS THAT RACIST"
READ WHAT YOU JUST TYPED
OOPS I tripped over your charging cable and tore it, my bad.
Guess you can't send that tweet til morning.
May as well go the fuck to sleep.

The giant pang—OH MY GOD dude
Again with this 306 shit
Week after week after week after fucking week
YOU WON THE ELECTION*,
WE KNOW, IT'S BEEN A YEAR
And it feels like twice as long
Since I asked you to FUCKING SLEEP.

The seeds slumber beneath—
Wait, what "tapes"
Are there fucking TAPES??
IS COMEY GONNA—
THEN
WHY
DID
YOU
TWEET
THAT????
SHIT
SHIT
SHIT
SHIT
FUCKING
SHIT

The flowers doze oh goddammit GODDAMMIT
DID YOU JUST DECLARE NUCLEAR WAR IN A TWEET???
HOW THE FUCK ARE YOU NOT BANNED FOR THAT
COME ON @JACK
I need to go fix this right now so PLEASE GO THE F—
Ah shit he already respo—
LOOK I DON'T KNOW WHAT A DOTARD IS.
HOW ARE YOU CRAZIER THAN HE IS. FUCK.
GO TO SLEEP.

Count some sheep...
off you go ...
     at long fucking last ...
        to sleep.

At last, some peace and quiet.
Just me, a good book and **DING DONG**
Oh shit. Goddamn it. This fucking guy.
Oh well, take me away. No more meltdowns. No more tweets.
Maybe I, too, can finally get some fucking sleep.

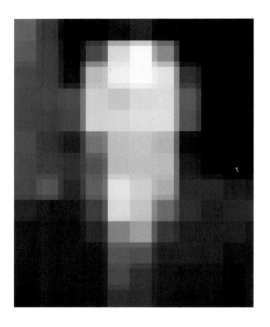

About the Author

John Spreincer McKellyanne Huckamucci is ███████████ ██ ███████ hopes to have a career in cable news one day. ██████████ lives in ███████████ ., and this is ████ first book.